STEM STARS

Women Who Rocked SPACE

Parragon

Bath • New York • Cologne • Melbourne • Delhi
Hong Kong • Shenzhen • Singapore

D1111842

This edition published by Parragon Books Ltd in 2017 and distributed by

Parragon Inc.
440 Park Avenue South, 13th Floor
New York, NY 10016
www.parragon.com

Written by Heather Alexander
Edited by Jeanine Le Ny
Art Direction by Andrew Barthelmes
Designed by Keith Plechaty

With thanks to Susan Lurie Ink, Inc.

ISBN 978-1-4748-9203-2

Printed in China

Picture Credits:
t = top, b = bottom

© NASA:
cover, 6b, NASA/David C. Bowman 10t, 10b, NASA/ESA/Hubble 11, 12,
NASA/EAS/Hubble 13, NASA/James Blair 15, 16t, NASA/MIT Museum
16b, 17,18b, 19-20, 23b, 24-25, NASA/JPL-Caltech/SSI 26b, 27, 28-29,
30b, 32-33, 35, 36-37, 39, 40-41, 42

© Shutterstock.com:
Sean Locke Photography 4t, D1min 4b, AstroStar 5, BeataGFX 19, Joe
Belanger/Shutterstock.com 31, Paulo Afonso/Shutterstock.com 38b

© Creative Commons
Eric S. Kounce/CC-BY-SA-3.0 7, RIA Novosti archive, image #619146/
Alexander Mokletsov/CC-BY-SA 3.0 14t, RIA Novosti archive, image
#17060/V. Malyshev/CC-BY-SA 3.0 14b, Rogerv W. Haworth/CC-BY-
SA-2.0 18t, John D. and Catherine T. MacArthur Foundation/CC-BY-4.0
30t, Victor R. Ruiz/CC-BY-2.0 38t

U.S. Geological Survey/photo by Jonathan Blair 22b, Caltech 26t, Jane
Luu 34, ESO/M. Kornmesser 43, Smithsonian Institution Archives. Image
Acc. 90-105 8b

Public Domain: 6t, 8t, 9, 11, 18t, 22t

Contents

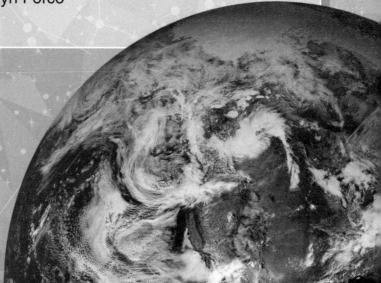

Introduction

"Science is not a boy's game. It's not a girl's game.
It's everyone's game."

—Nichelle Nichols

Do you ever look up at the night sky and wonder what lies beyond Earth? Since the beginning of time, humans have been curious about the stars. We've created stories about their patterns. We've used them to tell time and to get directions. They've inspired inventions to bring us closer to the worlds beyond.

Whether hurtling through the atmosphere or gazing through a telescope, amazing women have devoted their lives to understanding the mysteries of space. For a long time, only men were allowed to search the stars, but some awesome women wouldn't give up on their dreams to uncover the secrets of the universe, too.

The trailblazing women in this book are intelligent, strong, brave, and, most of all, curious. They broke barriers, made discoveries, and set

records. And you, too, can do what they did and more—reaching for even farther stars and galaxies yet to be explored.

Looking up!

✳ Our solar system has eight known planets. A planet orbits, or travels around, a star. The planets in our solar system are: Mercury, Venus, Earth, Mars, Jupiter, Saturn, Uranus, and Neptune. They orbit the Sun.

✳ All of the planets, except Mercury and Venus, have moons. Moons orbit around planets. Earth has one moon, but other planets have many moons.

✳ Stars, comets, asteroids, meteoroids, and dwarf planets are also in our solar system.

✳ A galaxy is a big collection of gas, dust, and billions of stars and their solar systems. It is held together by gravity. Our galaxy is called the Milky Way. There are many other galaxies beyond ours, waiting for us to find them!

Use the first letter of each word in this phrase to remember the order of the planets in our solar system:

My **Very** **Educated** **Mother** **Just** **Served** **Us** **Nachos.**

> "We especially need imagination in science. It is not all mathematics, nor all logic, but it is somewhat beauty and poetry." —Maria Mitchell

Maria Mitchell loved looking at the stars. Every night, she would climb to the roof of her house to "sweep the sky" with her father's telescope. She loved the beauty of the stars as much as the science behind charting their positions. It was this love that would lead her to incredible achievements—ones that other curious women would build upon for many years to come.

Thanks, Dad!

Maria Mitchell was born in 1818 on Nantucket Island in Massachusetts, back when it was the whaling capital of the world. Maria's dad was a school teacher and a banker, and he also worked on marine chronometers. Chronometers helped sailors use the Sun and stars to measure their locations at sea. Mr. Mitchell noticed Maria's early interest in the stars. He taught Maria all about chronometers, telescopes, and astronomy.

Maria didn't always follow the "rules" of the time—like not letting her female students go outside at night. How else would they see comets like this one?

Miss Mitchell's Comet

Mitchell

An asteroid and a crater of the Moon are also named after Maria!

After Maria finished school, she worked as a librarian. Each day she would read the library's books, and at night she'd gaze at the stars through a telescope. One night in 1847, Maria was observing the stars, when she spotted what seemed like a new comet. Her father wanted to announce her discovery right away, but Maria had to be sure. For the next two nights, she carefully recorded its position and made observations. It was true! Maria really *had* discovered a new comet!

This was a huge achievement. The comet became known as "Miss Mitchell's Comet," and Maria became the first professional female astronomer in the United States. The king of Denmark, who liked astronomy, awarded Maria a gold medal. She became the first woman elected to the American Academy of Arts and Sciences. In 1865, Maria became a professor at Vassar College. There, she continued her work with planetary and solar astronomy, making new discoveries on her own and with her students.

WHOA!

★ At 12, Maria calculated the position of her family's house during an eclipse.

★ Maria was against slavery. She refused to wear cotton grown by slaves.

★ It took almost 100 years before another woman joined Maria in the American Academy of Arts and Sciences!

Annie Jump Cannon

"Oh, Be A Fine Girl—Kiss Me!"
—Annie Jump Cannon

"How many stars are there?" Annie Jump Cannon would ask her mom as they stared up at the night sky. Her mother couldn't tell her. No one could. So, when Annie grew up, she created a way to count and organize the stars. Her system is still used today.

Mapping the Stars

Annie Jump Cannon was born in Delaware in 1863. Both her parents encouraged her love of learning, but her mother taught her about the stars. At Wellesley College in Massachusetts, Annie studied physics and astronomy. When she heard that Radcliffe College had state-of-the-art telescopes, she signed up for graduate classes. Harvard Observatory's director Edward C. Pickering soon hired Annie to be part of a group of women called the "Harvard Computers." At that time, "computers" weren't machines. They were people who did calculations!

Scarlet fever left Annie deaf. She didn't let it slow her down. In fact, she said the silence helped her concentrate.

Pickering hired only women. He thought they were better at details than men. He could also pay them half as much as men.

From Hot to Cool!

One of the jobs of the Harvard Computers was to map the stars. Annie didn't like the old, complicated system of organizing stars. Instead, she put them into groups based on their temperatures. She ranked the stars as O, B, A, F, G, K, or M. "O" was for the hottest stars and "M" for the coolest. The Sun is a "G" star. She created the saying, "Oh! Be A Fine Girl—Kiss Me!" to help astronomers remember the order of the letters. Using her system, Annie classified over 350,000 stars.

Annie was the first woman to receive the Draper Gold Medal from the National Academy of Sciences. She also received six honorary degrees, including the first one given to a woman from the University of Oxford in England. She died in 1941. In her honor every year, the American Astronomical Society gives the Annie Jump Cannon Award to an outstanding female astronomer.

WHOA!

✳ Annie was given the nickname "Census Taker of the Sky."

✳ People said Annie could look at any star and classify it in just 20 seconds!

✳ As a Harvard Computer, Annie made 25 cents per hour.

Katherine Johnson

". . . Anything that could be counted, I did." —Katherine Johnson

The United States was about to launch the first manned flight to orbit the Earth. Computers had calculated the flight plan, but astronaut John Glenn was nervous. If the numbers were off by even a little, he wouldn't make it back. He needed Katherine Johnson.

Math Whiz

Katherine Johnson always loved numbers. Born in 1918 in a small town in West Virginia, Katherine was doing high school math by age 10. No schools in her town taught African-American children past eighth grade, so her father moved the family to a town 125 miles away where she could continue her education. Katherine graduated college early at age 18 and became a teacher. Later, she heard that NACA—the National Advisory Committee for Aeronautics—was hiring African-American women who were good at math.

Being a woman at NASA wasn't easy back then. For one thing, women weren't included in meetings. That was, until Katherine asked, "Why not?"

There, she worked with a group of female "calculators," who checked the male engineers' math. The women were called "math whizzes in skirts."

Why Not?

Right away, Katherine stood out. While the other calculators worked quietly, Katherine asked lots of questions. She wanted to know "how" and "why" and then "why not." One day, Katherine was asked to help an all-male flight research team. They were so impressed with her math skills, they insisted she continue to work with them.

In 1957, the launch of the Soviet satellite *Sputnik* changed history. NACA soon formed into NASA—the National Aeronautics and Space Administration. By 1961, Katherine was working on the course of the first American flight into space. In 1962, NASA used computers to calculate John Glenn's orbit of Earth. Still, he insisted Katherine check the numbers. "If she says they're good, then I'm ready to go," Glenn said. He trusted her brain more than the machines! Katherine's groundbreaking work, including calculations that landed the first people on the Moon, continued for over 30 years, and she has received many honors and awards for her work.

At the age of 97, Katherine was awarded the Presidential Medal of Freedom by U.S. President Barack Obama.

Nancy Roman

> "Looking through the atmosphere is somewhat like looking through a piece of old, stained glass."
>
> —Nancy Roman

Nancy Roman was excited about the astronomy club she started with the other 11-year-old girls in her neighborhood, but after a while her friends moved on to different activities. Not Nancy. Her love for astronomy glowed brightly her whole life—and led her to become the first chief of astronomy at NASA.

Keep Going

Nancy Roman was born in Nashville, Tennessee, in 1925, but her family moved around a lot for her father's job as a geologist. No matter where she lived, Nancy always found herself looking up at the Moon and stars. When she started seventh grade, she announced she wanted to be an astronomer. Her mother warned her that this wouldn't be easy, since few women were in the field. But Nancy was determined. Her high school guidance counselor tried to talk her out of taking more math classes, saying

NASA's Hubble Space Telescope launched into space in 1990. It continues to help modern scientists understand the universe.

The Hubble Space Telescope captured this "butterfly nebula" in 2009. It's one of Nancy's favorite Hubble images.

girls didn't need math. But Nancy didn't listen. Many of her college professors thought she should stop studying and get married instead. Still, Nancy continued studying.

In Focus

Nancy did research at the University of Chicago. She discovered one of the first clues to how the Milky Way was formed. Next, she worked at the Naval Research Laboratory. Then NASA asked her to start their first space astronomy program in 1958. As part of her job, Nancy traveled around the United States to see what astronomers needed from the new space agency. She learned that they were having trouble getting clear, sharp images of space. Earth's atmosphere made the pictures blurry. Nancy took action. She gathered a group of engineers to develop the first orbiting telescope. It was called the Hubble Space Telescope. Since it orbited above the atmosphere, instead of being based on land, Hubble could transmit super-clear views of the universe back to Earth!

Nancy grew up to be exactly what she wanted to be—an amazing astronomer. After she retired, she enjoyed encouraging kids to love science and to dream big.

WHOA!

★ NASA called Nancy the "Mother of Hubble."

★ Every 97 minutes, the Hubble completes a spin around the Earth.

> "Anyone who has spent any time in space will love it for the rest of their lives." —Valentina Tereshkova

The bigger the jump, the bigger the thrill. That was what Valentina Tereshkova always believed. In school, she joined a parachute club and completed 126 jumps. Valentina was fearless. It was no wonder the Soviet Union chose her to become the first woman in space!

Her Turn

Valentina Tereshkova was born in 1937 in a village in western Russia. Her father was killed during World War II, and her mother worked in a cotton mill to support Valentina and her two siblings. Valentina left school at age 16 to help her mother in the mill. Whenever she had free time, Valentina would parachute.

Valentina became "the Hero of the Soviet Union" and signed lots of autographs. She wanted to go into space again, but unfortunately it never happened.

After Yuri Gagarin became the first man in space in 1961, the Soviet Union decided to send a woman next. Valentina didn't know how to fly an aircraft yet, but she *did* know how to jump out of one! She and four other women were chosen for space training. In the end, Valentina was selected.

Round and Round

On June 16, 1963, Valentina was launched in the *Vostok 6* spacecraft. Her flight lasted 2 days, 22 hours, and 50 minutes, and her spacecraft circled the Earth 48 times. Yuri Gagarin had orbited Earth only once, and the four male American astronauts who flew before Valentina had orbited 36 times combined. She had set a world record!

These days, safe landings include using parachute systems attached to spacecraft, not to astronauts!

When it was time to head home, though, Valentina noticed a problem. The ship was moving *away* from Earth instead of toward it. Quickly, she notified the Soviet scientists. Then she manually entered data to fix the navigation software. All that was left to do was jump from the space capsule before it hit the ground and parachute 20,000 feet down to safety. No problem for Valentina!

Margaret Hamilton

"There was no choice but to be pioneers." —Margaret Hamilton

On July 20, 1969, Neil Armstrong became the first person to walk on the Moon. Without Margaret Hamilton, though, he might never have taken those historic steps.

Girl Code

Margaret Hamilton was a self-taught computer programmer. Born in 1936 in Indiana, she majored in math at Earlham College. She got a job at the MIT Instrumentation Lab, where she was put in charge of a team picked by NASA. They would write guidance software for the in-flight computers to land the first humans on the Moon. This was the very beginning of computer programming. There were no laptops or home computers. The 70-pound computer aboard the Apollo 11 lunar module *Eagle* was the first "portable" computer. There were no earlier computer programs to learn from, so Margaret and her team had to create every command based on their knowledge of math.

Margaret spent years writing the code for the Moon landing. She programmed for all of the missions in the Apollo program.

Margaret's programming for the Moon landing pioneered the field of computer science!

The computer on the lunar module needed to be able to keep track of speed, location, and other data—and signal if there were problems. Margaret tested each program over and over again. Some people thought she tested too much and installed too many back-ups. But Margaret insisted. "There was no second chance," she said.

Warning!

Three minutes before the lunar module was about to land on the Moon, alarms rang. An error message showed that the landing software wouldn't work because the computer was overloaded. Should NASA tell the astronauts to turn around? Margaret knew what was wrong. The radar was flooding the computer with unnecessary data. Luckily, Margaret had thought ahead and installed a backup program that made the computer react to commands in the order of importance. Landing safely was definitely *most* important. And thanks to Margaret's programming, the astronauts did!

WHOA!

★ Ever hear the term "software engineering"? Margaret came up with that!

★ Margaret's young daughter crashed a command module simulator while playing with the keyboard—and discovered a fault in the program!

★ In 2016, Margaret was awarded the Presidential Medal of Freedom for her contributions to the space program.

Jocelyn Bell Burnell

> "... For me being a role model was quite an important one, just to show there are women doing science, enjoying it and being good at it."
>
> —Jocelyn Bell Burnell

Jocelyn Bell Burnell's father was an architect who designed a planetarium, and it sparked Jocelyn's interest in astronomy. She studied the stars—and went on to discover a new kind of star.

Something Strange

Jocelyn Bell Burnell was born in Belfast, Ireland in 1943. She studied physics in college and went to the University of Cambridge to get an advanced degree in radio astronomy. At Cambridge, she helped researcher Antony Hewish build a powerful radio telescope. Radio telescopes sense activity from radio wavelengths in space. Radio waves can travel very long distances between stars without being absorbed by thick clouds of gas and dust. Jocelyn

The blue dot is a pulsar. *Pulsar* is a blend of the words "pulsating" and "star."

was in charge of operating the radio telescope and looking at its data. Every four days, the telescope spat out radio wave markings onto hundreds of sfeet of paper. Then, on just one inch of the paper, Jocelyn noticed something strange.

A New Kind of Star

A radio source was making pulses faster than she'd ever seen. She showed Antony the strange markings. They soon realized that Jocelyn had discovered a pulsar—a new kind of neutron star. The core of this kind of star spins incredibly fast. As the star and its magnetic field whip through space, they release super-quick pulses of radiation.

Antony, Jocelyn, and a researcher named Martin Ryle published their findings in *Nature* magazine. In 1974, Antony and Martin won the Nobel Prize in Physics for having made one of the greatest astronomical discoveries. Jocelyn was left out. Why? Many scientists felt that she was treated unfairly because she was a woman. Others said it was because she was only a graduate student at the time.

When Jocelyn and her team first discovered the pulsing signal, they joked about it coming from space aliens. They nicknamed the pulsar LGM (Little Green Men).

Jocelyn received many other awards and honors, and she has spent her life teaching astrophysics at top universities.

Sally Ride

"The thing I'll remember most about the flight is that it was fun."

—Sally Ride

When Sally Ride was a girl watching the early space missions on TV, she never once thought that she would fly into space, too. Back then the space program was closed to girls. But soon, Sally would do something she never dreamed possible. She would become the first American woman to soar into space!

The Rules Change

Sally was born in 1951 in Encino, California. In school, she focused on being the best at science and athletics. Later, she went to Stanford University and graduated with degrees in physics and English. She also got a PhD, doing research in astrophysics. Now she was Dr. Sally Ride, and she planned to become a teacher. That was before she saw the newspaper headline that changed her life: "NASA to Recruit Women."

As a mission specialist, Sally operated the shuttle's robotic arm to release satellites into orbit.

Sally started Sally Ride Science to help students—especially girls—follow their passion for STEM.

Thousands of women wanted to be astronauts. Sally was one of only six women to be picked! She trained for a year and became an expert pilot and then . . . an astronaut!

To the Stars!

In 1982, Sally was chosen to be a member of the crew on the space shuttle *Challenger*. The crew prepared for a full year in life-sized models of the shuttle.

Then, on June 18, 1983, the space shuttle *Challenger* launched from Kennedy Space Center in Florida, and Sally made history—twice! She was the first American woman to go into space and, at age 32, she was also the youngest-ever U.S. astronaut.

For six days, Sally and the crew traveled more than 2.5 million miles. In 1984, she flew on the space shuttle once more. After working for NASA, Sally became a professor and wrote books for kids. She also developed programs to help young people discover how awesome science is. Sally died on July 23, 2013, at the age of 61. Her work continues to inspire young explorers.

WHOA!

★ As a teenager, Sally was a nationally ranked tennis player!

★ The U.S. Navy named a research ship in her honor.

★ Sally received the Presidential Medal of Freedom.

Carolyn Shoemaker

"If you know your subject and are willing to work hard, you will be accepted."

—Carolyn Shoemaker

As a girl, Carolyn Shoemaker did not like science and had no interest in looking at the stars. She thought all astronomers were "old men in white beards, smoking pipes, and staring at the sky." Instead, she studied history, became a junior high school teacher, and raised three kids. Then the strangest thing happened—at age 51, Carolyn became an astronomer and went on to discover the most comets of any astronomer ever!

Carolyn and Gene with their asteroid-hunting telescope. After Gene died, a small bottle of his ashes was sent to the moon.

What to Do?

Carolyn Shoemaker was born in 1929 in New Mexico but soon moved to California. After earning college degrees in history and political science, she met an astrogeologist named Gene Shoemaker. An astrogeologist studies what planets, moons, asteroids, comets, and meteoroids are made of. Carolyn and Gene got married, and

Carolyn stayed home to take care of their kids. After their children grew up, Carolyn needed something else to do. But what? Gene suggested she help out in his lab, where they were figuring out the chances of certain asteroids hitting Earth.

New Discoveries

Carolyn loved the work—and she was good at it, too. She spent long nights searching images taken by powerful telescopes. Carolyn discovered her first comet in 1983. In total, she has discovered 32 comets and over 800 asteroids—more than anyone else.

Carolyn is best known for her co-discovery of the comet Shoemaker-Levy 9 in 1993. The comet was orbiting Jupiter. It was the first time a comet had been seen orbiting a planet and not the Sun. In 1994 the comet broke apart, and the pieces smashed into Jupiter, causing huge explosions. For the first time, scientists saw what happened when a comet slammed into a planet.

Carolyn put in about 100 search hours for each comet she found.

Carolyn continues to search the sky for asteroids and comets at Lowell Observatory in Arizona.

Mae Jemison

"Never be limited by other people's limited imaginations."

–Mae Jemison

Dancer or doctor? Growing up, Mae Jemison had trained in ballet, modern, jazz, and African and Haitian dance. But she wanted to be a doctor, too. Which should she choose? Her mother told her, "You can always dance if you're a doctor, but you can't doctor if you're a dancer." Mae listened to her mom, became a doctor, and went on to become the first African-American woman in space!

By the Book

Mae Jemison was born in Alabama in 1956, and her family moved to Chicago when she was three. As a girl, Mae always had her nose in a book. She'd take out piles of science and science fiction books from the Chicago library. She was such a good student that at age 16 she was already studying chemical engineering at Stanford University. She also learned to speak Russian, Japanese, and Swahili. She graduated medical school and became a doctor.

As a kid, Mae loved the character Lieutenant Uhura from the TV show *Star Trek*. Soon enough she'd be flying in space herself in the STS-47 *Endeavour*!

Mae stopped her work when the shuttle orbited over Chicago so she could see her hometown from high above Earth.

After Mae watched Sally Ride's historic space flight in 1983, she couldn't stop thinking about it. She called NASA and asked for an application form.

3-2-1 Liftoff!

Mae and 14 others were selected from 2,000 applications, and in 1987 she became the first African-American woman in the astronaut program. After more than a year of training, she was named Science Mission Specialist. She would be in charge of scientific experiments on the space shuttle. Mae launched into space on September 12, 1992, with six other astronauts aboard the space shuttle *Endeavour*. She was in space for eight days and orbited Earth 127 times.

Mae was busy during the flight conducting experiments. One experiment was on motion sickness. Over 80 percent of all astronauts feel nausea during space flight. Mae tested herself and other crew members to find out if breathing techniques could be more helpful than medicine. Mae retired from NASA in 1993. She now leads 100 Year Starship, a government-funded project to develop a plan for interstellar travel.

WHOA!

★ Mae was once a Peace Corps medical officer in Sierra Leone and Liberia.

★ Mae used to be afraid of heights! When she got into the astronaut training program, she mentally willed herself to overcome it.

Carolyn Porco

> "We humans, though troubled and warlike, are also the dreamers, thinkers, and explorers inhabiting one achingly beautiful planet."
>
> —Carolyn Porco

When she was a teenager, Carolyn Porco's friend invited her up to her roof to look through her telescope. Carolyn was only mildly interested . . . until she found Saturn in the night sky. In that moment, she felt a thrill—as if she were the first person to discover Saturn. She knew then that this magical ringed planet would be forever in her life.

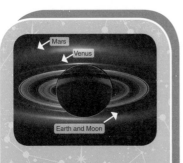

On July 19, 2013, *Cassini* snapped a picture of Earth. Carolyn called it "The Day the Earth Smiled." From Saturn, we look like a tiny dot.

Passion for Planets

Born in 1953, Carolyn Porco grew up in New York City, where the bright lights made viewing stars tricky. While studying astronomy in college, she realized her passion was for planets more than stars, so she got her PhD in Geological and Planetary Sciences.

Carolyn became a member of the Voyager Imaging Team in 1983. *Voyager I* and *II* were unmanned spacecraft that explored Jupiter, Saturn, Neptune, Uranus, and the outer solar system. Carolyn examined the imaging data they transmitted to Earth. Her first big discovery came when dark markings, called spokes, were spotted on the rings around Saturn. Carolyn was the first to relate them to Saturn's magnetic field. Then she helped discover that Neptune also has rings.

WHOA!

* Carolyn co-wrote over 120 scientific papers about astronomy and planetary science.

* Carolyn produced two space documentaries. She was also an adviser for the movies *Contact* (1997) and *Star Trek* (2009).

Smile and Say "Saturn!"

Carolyn was chosen to be the leader of the Imaging Science Team for NASA's Cassini Mission around Saturn. The nuclear-powered robotic spacecraft was the size of a bus. It arrived at Saturn in 2004 and finished its mission in 2017. Carolyn and her team discovered seven moons and also found new rings. But the most exciting discovery was that Enceladus—a moon of Saturn—may

Carolyn invited everyone on Earth to wave at Saturn as their picture was taken from hundreds of millions of miles away. About 1,600 people sent pictures of themselves waving.

be able to support life! Carolyn and her team spotted over 100 tall geysers erupting from its south pole. They believe the geysers come from a salty ocean or sea deep under the moon's surface. Carolyn thinks a probe should be sent to investigate this further. Carolyn has received many awards and honors for her work.

Ellen Ochoa

> "Only you put limitations on yourself about what you can achieve so don't be afraid to reach for the stars."
>
> —Ellen Ochoa

Ellen Ochoa learned the importance of hard work from her mom. Mrs. Ochoa raised Ellen and her four siblings on her own while working full time and taking college classes at night. Ellen vowed that she, too, would work hard to achieve what she wanted—and she did. She became the world's first Latina astronaut.

Hard Worker

Ellen Ochoa was born in 1958 in California. She was excellent at math and science, and she loved to play the flute. Although Ellen was offered a scholarship to Stanford University, she went to San Diego State so she could stay close to home to help care for her brothers and sisters. She worked hard and graduated first in her college class. Afterward, she went to Stanford to get her master's degree and PhD in electrical engineering.

Before becoming an astronaut, Ellen considered a career as a musician. She brought her flute aboard the shuttle to play for her crewmates.

Ellen and the other crew members of the space shuttle *Atlantis* were expected to know the function of every part of the shuttle.

Ellen had never once thought about becoming an astronaut. Then, when she was in graduate school, she heard that Sally Ride had orbited the Earth. Ellen was fascinated. If Sally Ride could go into space, could she go, too? She applied to NASA, but they didn't take her. So Ellen concentrated on electrical engineering. She worked hard and became a successful researcher in optics, the study of light.

Lucky Number Three

Ellen refused to give up on becoming an astronaut, though. She applied to NASA again and again. The third time, she got in.

In 1993, she flew on the space shuttle *Discovery*. She was a mission specialist and was in charge of working a gigantic robotic arm to release a satellite to study the Sun. She flew three more space missions in 1994, 1999, and 2002, logging 978 hours in space.

Ellen is now the director of the Johnson Space Center in Houston, Texas—the second woman to hold this title. Even though she's flown four missions in space, she keeps on working hard!

WHOA!

★ Ellen has at least five schools named after her!

★ She co-invented three systems that improve the quality of pictures taken from space.

★ Ellen video-chatted with her two sons while she was up in space!

Andrea Ghez

"Once you've started to do work on one question, what you find is not only the answer to the first question but often new puzzles."

—Andrea Ghez

Andrea Ghez loves puzzles—jigsaw puzzles, crossword puzzles, Sudoku puzzles—all kinds of puzzles. The mysteries of the universe, she says, are just another kind of puzzle to solve. And Andrea filled in a big missing piece of that puzzle—she proved the existence of a black hole at the center of our galaxy.

Andrea used the twin Keck telescopes in Hawaii for her black hole research. They are the largest telescopes in the world.

A View of the Stars

Andrea Ghez wanted to be a ballet dancer until she watched the first Moon landing on TV in 1969, when she was four years old. Then she wanted to explore outer space. Her parents bought her a telescope, but Chicago's city skies weren't clear enough to see much. When she was studying physics at the Massachusetts Institute of Technology (MIT), she got her first real view of the stars through the university's high-power telescope—and that's when she knew she wanted to be an astronomer.

It's Dark Out There

Andrea is best known for her research on black holes. A black hole sucks up debris in outer space like a vacuum, using gravity to pull everything in. The gravity in a black hole is so strong that it can even suck up light—and light travels at the speed of 186,000 miles per second!

Andrea wanted to know if there was a black hole at the center of the Milky Way. It is impossible to see a black hole directly, because it's completely dark. However, Andrea discovered that if the black hole is near a bright object, like a star, observing the star's orbit could help unlock the secrets of the black hole. For ten years, she measured the movement of stars. Finally she was able to prove the existence of a supermassive black hole, known as Sagittarius A*, at the center of our galaxy.

Andrea is an award-winning professor of astronomy and a public speaker. She continues to search for the missing puzzle pieces to our understanding of space.

WHOA!

✴ Sagittarius A* is about four million times bigger than our Sun!

✴ Andrea used to be afraid of speaking in front of others. Now she turns her nervousness into excitement.

✴ Andrea has won the Annie Jump Cannon Award in Astronomy, among others.

This drawing shows of the activity at the center of our Milky Way galaxy, and where Sagittarius A* is located.

Eileen Collins

> ## "My daughter just thinks that all moms fly the space shuttle."
> —Eileen Collins

Eileen Collins sat on the roof of her family's car and watched the gliders take off at the local airport. She was in third grade, and she dreamed of flying airplanes. Eileen also dreamed of becoming an astronaut, but she kept that dream a secret. She thought people would laugh. There were no girl astronauts back then. But as Eileen grew up, she never let go of her dream . . . and one day, she would live it.

At the Controls

Eileen was born in 1956, in Elmira, New York. Her family never seemed to have enough money. Eileen disliked living on welfare and food stamps, and she vowed to succeed and make her family proud. Having earned her pilot's license at age 19, she entered the pilot training course at Oklahoma's Vance Air Force Base after college. Her class was one

Eileen was always busy on her missions. She said once that she'd like to experience a flight as a tourist so that she could just enjoy being in space.

Eileen was the first to fly a space shuttle into a back flip! Why? So astronauts could check the bottom of the shuttle for damage.

of the first to include women. She flew military cargo planes, completed advanced degrees at Stanford University and Webster University, and then was accepted at the U.S. Air Force Test Pilot School at Edwards Air Force Base. Test pilots are chosen from the U.S. Air Force's best and brightest pilots, navigators, and engineers. They are trained to test new aircraft and to fly test missions. In 1990, she became only the second woman to graduate as a test pilot. She logged over 5,000 hours in 30 different types of aircraft. But Eileen still had her dream of becoming an astronaut. She applied to NASA.

First! First! First!

Eileen became an astronaut in 1991 and was the first woman to undergo the Space Shuttle Program's pilot training. In 1995, she made history by becoming the first woman to pilot a space shuttle, serving as second-in-command of *Discovery*. She made a second flight as a pilot, and in 1999, she became the first female commander of a space shuttle mission. That's a lot of firsts!

WHOA!

★ During high school Eileen worked at a pizza parlor to save up the money needed for her first flying lessons.

★ She went on four missions and logged over 872 hours in space.

★ Eileen is in the National Women's Hall of Fame.

Jane Luu

> "If you're interested in something, you're already halfway there."
>
> —Jane Luu

For many years, astronomers wondered if there was anything in space beyond Pluto, or was it just dark and empty? Astronomer Jane Luu answered the question—and forever changed how we think about our solar system.

Planets!

Jane was born in South Vietnam in 1963. Her father was an interpreter for the U.S. military. When Jane was almost 12, her family had to flee the Vietnam War for safety. They lived in a refugee camp before moving to Kentucky with Jane's aunt. Jane didn't speak any English, but she did speak French. In school, she carried a French-English dictionary. Jane graduated at the top of her high school class, majored in physics at Stanford University, and then got a job at the Jet Propulsion Laboratory. Walking down the halls there, she loved looking at the close-up pictures of planets. That was when Jane decided to become an astronomer.

Researchers have used Jane's discovery of KBOs to improve understanding of planet formation.

Keep Looking

Jane was paired with adviser David Jewitt at MIT for graduate work. They focused on space beyond Neptune. What was out there? In 1951, astronomer Gerard Kuiper had said that debris left over from the formation of our solar system—about 4.6 billion years ago—probably existed beyond the known solar system. He called this debris Kuiper Belt Objects, or KBOs. Most scientists agreed that KBOs *had* existed but thought they were long gone. Jane and David weren't so sure.

For five years, they searched with high-power telescopes and found nothing. People thought they were crazy, but Jane and David continued on. After they started using huge telescopes at the top of Mauna Kea in

Astronomers used to think that Pluto was a planet in our solar system. After Jane's discovery, they realized that it is actually a *dwarf* planet and a big KBO. Sorry, Pluto!

Hawaii, they made their big discovery. Jane and David spotted the first Kuiper Belt Object in 1992, expanding the borders of the solar system for the first time since the discovery of Pluto in 1930, and encouraging others to push further. Since then, thousands of KBOs have been found thanks to Jane!

Sunita Williams

"Looking down at the Earth, we could not see borders or people with different nationalities . . . all of us are citizens of the universe."

—Sunita Williams

On your mark, get set, go! In 2007, runners sprinted into the streets to start the 26.2-mile Boston Marathon. Sunita Williams began to run, too, except her feet weren't pounding the pavement. Sunita was a NASA astronaut up in the International Space Station (ISS), orbiting Earth at 17,500 miles per hour. Strapped to a treadmill to fight weightlessness, Sunita crossed the orbital finish line after 4 hours, 24 minutes. She was the first astronaut to complete a marathon in space.

To train for the ISS, Sunita spent nine days in the Aquarius underwater lab. "It is a good test to see how you like living in a can," she said.

On the Move

Sunita Williams, known as "Sunny" around the Johnson Space Center, was born in Ohio in 1965. Sunita competed on swim teams and loved being outdoors. She planned to be a veterinarian, but her older brother convinced her to join him at the U.S. Naval Academy.

So far, Sunita holds the record for total spacewalk time by a woman (50 hours, 40 minutes).

Sunita became a helicopter pilot and served in the Mediterranean, Red Sea, and Persian Gulf in Operation Desert Shield during the Gulf War. At the U.S. Naval Test Pilot School, she logged over 3,000 flight hours in more than 30 different aircraft. When her class visited the Johnson Space Center, Sunita was fascinated. She learned that NASA accepted helicopter pilots as astronauts because they could fly vertical landing crafts. She sent in her application right away.

Setting a Record

Sunita's first space flight was aboard the shuttle *Discovery* as part of the 14th expedition to the ISS in 2006. She stayed in space for 195 days—at that point, the longest time for any female astronaut. Sunita returned to space in 2012 as the commander of ISS Expedition 32/33—only the second woman to do so. She still works for NASA and is training to be one of the first astronauts to fly America's first commercial space flight.

WHOA!

★ The movie *Top Gun* inspired Sunita to become a Navy pilot.

★ While on the ISS, Sunita donated her ponytail to Locks of Love by sending it to Earth via space shuttle.

★ During her second mission on the ISS, Sunita completed a triathlon in space.

Jill Tarter

"... If we never search, the chance for success is zero."   —Jill Tarter

When Jill Tarter was a young girl, she and her dad would walk along the Florida beaches at night and look up at the stars. Jill thought of all the other girls around the world gazing at the same stars. Did they wonder who lived up there, too? Did they believe that humans weren't alone in the universe? It's not surprising that Jill grew up to become a scientist who searches for aliens!

Hello? Anyone Out There?

Born in 1944 in upstate New York, Jill Tarter decided to become an engineer at eight years old. Years later, at Cornell University, she discovered that out of 300 engineering students, she was the only woman. It was tough, but Jill liked that every professor knew who she was. After Cornell, she finished a master's degree and PhD in astronomy at the University of California, Berkeley. In the 1970s, a group of NASA researchers began developing radio equipment to look for other forms of life in the universe. Jill had taught herself

Jill had said that if SETI captured a real signal from outer space, they would *not* reply— unless the world agreed that they should and figured out who should speak for Earth.

to program the computer they were using, so they asked her to join them. Jill was hooked!

Scanning the Skies

Jill became the director of the Center for SETI Research. (SETI is short for Search for Extraterrestrial Intelligence.) Astronomers use radio telescopes to search the skies for special radio wave patterns that might have been sent by other civilizations in space.

WHOA!

✴ Jill was the inspiration for the main character in Carl Sagan's novel *Contact*, which was made into a movie.

✴ An alien message would have to travel thousands, if not millions, of years to get from planet to planet.

Radio waves can travel the great distances between stars. Alien signals haven't been found yet, but the universe is huge. Jill once said, "The amount of searching that we've done in 50 years is equivalent to scooping one 8-ounce glass out of the Earth's ocean, looking and seeing if you caught a fish. I don't think you're going to conclude that there are no fish in the ocean."

Jill has received many awards and honors for her work. She retired from leading SETI in 2012 and has turned her focus toward raising money to keep the research going.

Jill was in charge of the Allen Telescope Array project in California that used many antennas in Australia, Puerto Rico, and West Virginia to survey a million stars.

Peggy Whitson

"Think about it. If you had been up there, wouldn't you want to go back?"

—Beth Whitson, Peggy's mom

Home, sweet, home . . . that's how Peggy Whitson thinks of the International Space Station. She went there three times! And she was its first female commander. She topped the record for any American—male or female—for time in space, breaking the previous record of 534 days held by Jeff Williams.

Never Give Up

Peggy Whitson was born in 1960, in Iowa, and grew up on a farm. When she was nine, she watched the first Moon landing on TV and decided she'd be an astronaut, too. To earn money for flying lessons, she raised and sold chickens for $2.00 each. Peggy's college professors said she should go to medical school, but Peggy wanted to be a space scientist. After getting a PhD in biochemistry, she worked at the Johnson Space

Peggy grew a crop of Chinese cabbage aboard the ISS. The crew saved some for research and then ate the rest!

Peggy trained underwater for her spacewalks at the Neutral Buoyancy Lab at Johnson Space Center.

Center. For ten years she applied to be an astronaut and kept getting turned down. But Peggy didn't give up— and finally she was picked!

Peggy flew her first mission to the ISS in 2002 as part of Expedition 5. In 2008, she went up again as part of Expedition 16 and became its first female commander. She spent 377 days in space on those missions, making her NASA's most experienced female astronaut. Back on Earth, Peggy became the first woman to be Chief of the Astronaut Office. She was in charge of choosing and preparing the astronauts to work at the ISS. But Peggy couldn't keep her feet on the ground. In 2016, she joined Expedition 50/51 for her third mission in space.

Experiments!

Peggy did lots of different experiments in space. For example, she helped design a new water filtration system that's used in hospitals. She tested solutions of iron that will someday be used to build suspension bridges. And she researched how the body functions without gravity to help plan for missions to Mars!

WHOA!

★ At age 56, Peggy was the oldest woman to blast off into space.

★ In space, Peggy's favorite food is peanut butter—but not on Earth. It tastes different up there!

Debra Fischer

> ### "The search for planets is the search for life."
> —Debra Fischer

For a very long time, many scientists believed that the eight planets that orbited the Sun were the only planets in the universe. Then they began to look beyond our solar system. In 1995, the first exoplanet was discovered. Exoplanet is short for extrasolar planet—a planet that orbits a star other than the Sun. Debra Fischer hunts for exoplanets. In fact, many say she's the best exoplanet hunter of all.

New Solar Systems

Debra Fischer was born in 1951 in Iowa. In college, she studied physics, planning to go to medical school. Then she took her first astronomy class, and the beauty of the subject changed her mind. She got her PhD in astrophysics and was invited to join one of the first teams searching for exoplanets.

Debra uses wavelengths of light from distant stars to look for

This is what the surface might look like on exoplanet Proxima b, which orbits the closest star to our solar system. Scientists hope to learn if the planet can support life!

exoplanets. Changes in the wavelengths show that a nearby orbiting planet may be tugging at the star. One of Debra's first important discoveries was that the star Upsilon Andromedae has three planets orbiting it.

For the first time, astronomers had proof that a star similar to our Sun was orbited by a family of planets!

The Search for "Goldilocks"

NASA launched the space telescope Kepler in 2009 to look for exoplanets. Kepler is able to spot a dip in a star's brightness when an exoplanet travels in front of it. However, Debra and her team are now working on creating powerful instruments that can show them more. They are searching for a "Goldilocks planet"—a planet that is "just right" for life to exist.

This kind of planet, like Earth, would have liquid water on it. This means it has to be the right distance from its star so that its temperature is not too hot and not too cold!

In addition to being a planet hunter, Debra is a Professor of Astronomy at San Francisco State University.

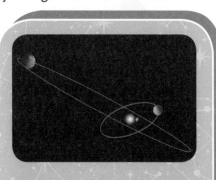

The Andromedae system showed astronomers that other solar systems may not work the same way ours does.

Out-of-This-World Careers

Whether you want to blast into orbit in a space shuttle, gaze at galaxies through powerful telescopes, supervise science experiments at a space station, or build machines to journey to faraway worlds, so many stellar career choices await you.

If you want to stay on Earth . . .

★ **Astronomers** study the universe and the objects in it. Some study planets, and some study stars. They use powerful telescopes to collect data to understand how the universe was created and how it has changed.

★ **Astrobiologists** study how life forms and develops. They try to find out if life does or can exist elsewhere in space, and they search for habitable planets around other stars.

★ **Astrophysicists** use physics and chemistry to explain the birth, life, and death of stars, planets, galaxies, and other objects in the universe.

Classes you will take	math, science, and computer science
Places you can work	observatories, research laboratories, universities
What you can do now	join a local astronomy club, visit a planetarium

★ **Aerospace/Aeronautical Engineers and Computer Programmers** make space exploration travel possible. They design spacecraft, space vehicles, and space stations. They also create and program space satellites and figure out how to fly to the stars—and return home safely.

Classes you will take	math, biology, chemistry, physics, and computer science
Places you can work	government agencies such as NASA; private companies such as Boeing, Lockheed Martin, and SpaceX
What you can do now	play strategy games like chess and do puzzles, build with Legos, join a robotics club, learn to code

If you want to go into space . . .

* **Astronauts** are scientists, engineers, or pilots who are trained to fly in a spacecraft and explore space. They try to understand how space affects the human body.

Some astronaut jobs:

* The **commander** is the captain of the spacecraft or ISS and makes the decisions affecting the crew and the mission.

* The **pilot** is second-in-command. Both the commander and the pilot are responsible for the controls and the flight.

* The **mission specialist** is a scientist or an engineer who does experiments, launches satellites, and maintains equipment.

Classes you will take	a well-rounded education with a focus on science and math; flight school
Places you can work	NASA or a commercial space flight company
What you can do now	visit an airfield, become a strong swimmer, learn how to scuba dive, play a competitive sport

Glossary

Apollo Missions (1963-1973): A spaceflight program that placed the first humans on the Moon.

asteroid: A small rocky object that orbits the sun.

astronomy: The study of outer space.

astrophysics: The science used to explain the birth, life, and death of galaxies and other objects in the universe.

atmosphere: A layer of gases surrounding a planet.

census: An official count of a population.

comet: An object made up of gas, rock, and dust

commercial space flight: A flight into space that is paid for by a person or company.

crater: A round hole created on the surface of a moon or planet.

dwarf planet: An object in space that orbits a star and shares its orbit with other objects.

extraterrestrial: From outside Earth or its atmosphere.

geologist: A scientist who studies the Earth. Earth's structure, history, and forces.

geyser: A vent that spouts out water or steam.

gravity: A strong, invisible force that makes pieces of matter hold together.

interstellar: Happening or situated between stars.

Johnson Space Center: The control center for NASA's human space flight program.

lunar module: A part of an Apollo spacecraft that transported astronauts between the main craft and the Moon's surface.

meteoroid: A rock or space particle, similar to an asteroid but much smaller.

nebula: A cloud of gas and dust in space.

neutron star: The leftover part of a big star that exploded.

physics: The study of how matter and energy react to each other.

planetarium: A place where you can learn about stars and planets.

probe: A machine that sends data from space to Earth for scientists to study.

radio astronomy: Astronomy dealing with radio waves received from outside Earth's atmosphere.

radio wave: An invisible wave made when an electric field joins with a magnetic field. It travels at the speed of light.

satellite: A machine launched into space that orbits Earth or another object in space. It can take pictures, send TV signals, connect phone calls, track weather, and more.

solar eclipse: The passage of the Moon between the Earth and the Sun.

space shuttle: A reusable spacecraft that launches like a rocket and lands like an airplane.

spacewalk: Activity performed by an astronaut outside a spacecraft.

star: A ball of hot, glowing gas.

wavelength: Sound and light travel as invisible waves. The wavelength is the distance between each wave.

weightlessness: Floating because there is no gravity.

Index